Needle Painting Embroidery

FRESH IDEAS FOR BEGINNERS

Needle Painting Embroidery

FRESH IDEAS FOR BEGINNERS

TRISH BURR

SALLYMILNER
PUBLISHING

For Mum, Dad and Tess with thanks for all your help packing kits!

First published in 2011 by

Sally Milner Publishing Pty Ltd

734 Woodville Road

Binda NSW 2583 AUSTRALIA

© Trish Burr 2011

Reprinted in 2012

Design: Anna Warren, Warren Ventures

Editing: Anne Savage

Photography: Trish Burr

Printed in China

National Library of Australia Cataloguing-in-Publication data:

Author:	Burr, Trish.
Title:	Needle painting embroidery : fresh ideas for beginners / Trish Burr.
ISBN:	9781863514200 (pbk.)
Series:	Milner craft series.
Subjects:	Embroidery.
Dewey Number:	746.44028

Disclaimer

Information and instructions given in this book are presented in good faith, but no warranty is given nor results guaranteed, nor is freedom from any patent to be inferred. As we have no control over physical conditions surrounding application of information herein contained in this book, the author and publisher disclaim any liability for untoward results.

10 9 8 7 6 5 4 3

Acknowledgements

Take my life, and let it be
Consecrated, Lord, to Thee.
Take my moments and my days,
Let them flow in ceaseless praise.
Take my hands, and let them move
At the impulse of Thy love.
FRANCES R. HAVERGAL

As always my thanks go to Libby Renney and all the staff at Sally Milner who produce such wonderful publications. Grateful thanks to DMC in South Africa for donating all the stranded cotton for these projects. A big thank you to Merle Clarence and Frances Chittenden for making up the exquisite little pincushion, scissors case, pin-wheel and scissors fob—they really are stunning and I certainly couldn't have done it without you! Thanks to my Friday class, Anne, Rosemary, Merle, Jen, Roz and Helen, for their continuous support and critiques on my work. My special thoughts go to our dear friend Norma Young, who passed away recently and without whose prompting I would not have done half of what I do. Here's another book for your collection, Norma! To Leslie Ann, with thanks for all your advice and encouragement. To my husband Simon, who always supports my endeavours and patiently encourages my endless source of new ideas, and to my family: I love you lots.

Contents

THE PROJECTS   *33*

Level one projects

Introduction

As the 2010 Soccer World Cup climaxed in a frenzy of anticipation here in Cape Town, I couldn't help feeling the vibe—thousands of people from all around the world revelling in the atmosphere, the sound of vuvuzelas, the colourful flags, the face paint, smiling faces and soccer paraphernalia—all fostering an infectious good feeling. While many suffer the effects of a world recession I believe this event gave us a good excuse to briefly put aside our differences and problems and participate in the vibe. Isn't this what happens when we stitch? We transport ourselves into a realm of creativity and peace, so much better than Prozac!

Being a self-taught embroiderer I understand the need for clear instructions and have spent many hours exploring the simplest way to present project instructions so that they are simple to follow. The escalating cost of importing the materials from overseas into South Africa, where they incur massive customs duties, and the increasing expense of assembling project kits, means that making up individual kits is no longer feasible. I have therefore decided to provide instead project books containing the instructions from numerous kits, which I believe will offer added value.

Since all the projects use easily obtainable DMC/Anchor stranded cotton, you should find it relatively straightforward to put together the materials needed for each one. For those who prefer the design outline ready printed onto fabric I will continue to supply pre-printed fabric packs through my website or through the nearest stockist in your country. If you have any difficulty obtaining any of the materials please do not hesitate to contact me via my website, www.trishburr.co.za. I will be happy to help.

This book is aimed at the beginner who would like to learn the needle painting technique, but will also be helpful to those who have some experience but feel the need to work on their technique or who are looking for smaller designs to use for gifts. Intermediate to advanced

projects will be published in a later book, and of course can be sourced from any of my previous books.

Here I have provided information on the materials and preparation recommended for this style of embroidery, plus an introduction to long and short stitch, which is basically a hard copy of my DVD: The Long & The Short of It: A Needle Painting Workshop. You may wish to view this DVD, as it is very helpful to actually see the technique being stitched. Here you will find practice motifs for every situation that you may encounter in long and short stitch—basic, curved, different shapes and feathers. Be prepared to spend time on each one, as practice really does make perfect and it will save you a lot of heartache later on.

The projects in this book are divided into three levels, from complete beginner through to more intermediate embroiderers. Each level is carefully designed to take you onto the next stage of needle painting and includes all aspects of the technique. Each project has been worked personally, with many trips up and down the sixteen steps to my office as I scanned each stage of the stitching. Yes, I have counted those steps—I mention this because my family is testament to my muttering as I went up those steps yet again: 'I hope they appreciate this!' The seemingly sedentary task of needle painting literally keeps me on my toes and provides much-needed exercise, so thank you for that!

I trust that you will rapidly gain in confidence and become seriously addicted to shaded embroidery. Remember that no two artists paint the same picture, so if your work does not look exactly the same as the original, or the same as your neighbour's, that's okay—each piece is unique in itself and expresses its creator, and is beautiful in its own right.

These pages are dedicated to all of you, with my best wishes for blissful stitching.

TRISH BURR

Materials and preparation

FABRIC

The best type of fabric to use for this style of embroidery is either linen or cotton satin. By linen I mean good quality Irish or Belgian linen with a close weave, not the type available for counted thread embroidery. Cotton satin is a good cost-effective alternative and can be purchased by the piece on my website: www.trishburr.co.za

Alternatively, you can use a good quality batiste or high count quilter's cotton—again, it should have a smooth close weave. Batiste is very light weight so you should use a second piece as a backing fabric.

Irish and Belgian linen can be obtained online through these websites:

www.mariesuarez.com

www.communionlinens.com

www.maceandnairn.com

LINING UP THE FABRIC

It is important to make sure that your fabric is mounted in the hoop *with* the grain and not *against* it. To do this, pull a thread on two sides at right angles on the fabric.

Irish linen

Cotton satin

Lining up the fabric

If the linen is very fine you should use a backing fabric to support the embroidery. I use a fine batiste cotton, but a good quality lightweight calico is also suitable. Make sure that the fabric you buy does not have any stretch in it—try this out in the shop. Pull the fabric across the grain both ways. If it stretches, it will distort in the hoop and cause puckering.

Always leave an allowance of at least 5 cm (2 in) around the edge of the design to allow plenty of room for making up or framing.

THREAD

DMC stranded cotton or alternatives such as Anchor work best for needle painting embroidery. One strand is used throughout unless otherwise indicated.

All thread has a nap, which is the direction that the pile of the yarn lies. To keep your stitching smooth it helps to thread your needle with the strand in the same direction each time. An easy way to keep track of the direction you thread the yarn into the needle is to pull out a length of thread (I like to use about 60 cm / 24 in at a time), separate one strand and pull it out from the rest. Cut off this strand only and thread the top end through the needle. Each time you re-thread, pull out another strand and use the same end.

Selection of DMC stranded cottons

NEEDLES

Crewel embroidery needles numbers 9 and 10 are the needles to use—no. 9 for two strands and no, 10 for one strand. I prefer the good quality needles from the English firms Hemmings, Colonial or John James.

HOOPS AND FRAMES

The best hoop to use is a Susan Bates Super Grip embroidery hoop. This keeps your fabric drum tight, which is essential to avoid puckering. Always use a hoop that is a lot larger than the design you are working so that there is plenty of room to eliminate hoop marks. Otherwise you can use an artist's stretcher frame, which does not present the problem of hoop marks.

Richard Hemming & Son brand embroidery needles size 9; Susan Bates moulded plastic hoop

Magnifying lamp

Although magnifying lamps can be costly they are almost an essential and integral part of this style of embroidery. It will help you to see the fine details and save you a lot of frustration. If you cannot afford a magnifying lamp (such as the Daylight Slimline shown in the picture), get yourself a good quality craft lamp with a daylight bulb and a separate magnifier. You can also wear a pair of reader's specs on top of your prescription specs to magnify the work—but remember that good light is vital.

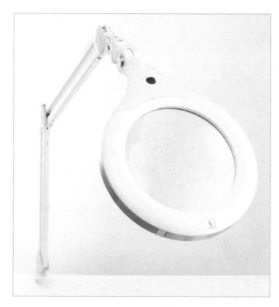

Adjustable magnifying lamp

Other items

❖ A sharp, good quality pair of embroidery scissors.

❖ An HB pencil for transferring the design and adding in direction lines.

Transferring the outline

To transfer the design onto your fabric, trace the outline onto a piece of tracing paper (or have it photocopied). Place the outline on a light box, or against a window, and tape it in place with masking tape. Place your fabric on top of this—find the centre of your fabric and again tape in place. Ensure that the fabric is taped tightly across with no wrinkles. With the light showing through you will easily be able to see the lines—trace over these lines with a pencil.

Adjustable craft lamp

An example of pre-printed fabric (for the apricot dahlia embroidery)

Pre-printed fabric Alternatively, you can purchase cotton satin fabric with a pre-printed outline on my website: www.trishburr.co.za

WHAT TO DO WITH THE COMPLETED STITCHING

If necessary you can wash your work in warm soapy water (a mild soap such as sunlight), then rinse thoroughly and roll up in a fluffy towel to absorb the bulk of the moisture. While still damp, iron the work face down on a fluffy towel with medium heat. If you have used cotton satin, be particularly careful not to allow the iron to get too hot, as the satin component will scorch.

You can mount the embroidery onto a piece of acid-free board, or take it to a good framer who will do it for you. Other ideas include making it up into a small cushion, needlecase, scissors fob, sachet, pincushion, book cover, cell phone case, bookmark or greeting card.

The smaller designs in level one make lovely gifts that are quick to stitch. Merle Clarence and Frances Chittenden of South Africa, both experts in their fields of quilting and embroidery, kindly made up the beautiful pincushion, scissors case, pin-wheel and scissors fob shown here.

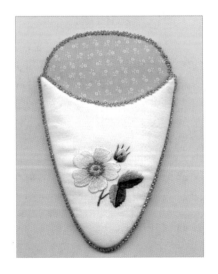   

Sunset alpine rose embroidery made up into a scissors case; Red alpine rose embroidery made up into a scissors fob; Golden yellow anemone embroidery made up into a pincushion; Cerise anemone embroidery made up into a pinwheel

Introducing long and short stitch

*L*ong and short stitch is a surface embroidery technique used to fill a motif with subtle shading. The shading is worked in rows of colour which softly blend into each other. It is often referred to as silk shading, soft shading, thread painting or needle painting, and can be done in cotton, silk or wool. Here are some examples of my work.

The King Protea (*Protea cynaroides*) is the largest protea. It is worked in one strand of DMC and Anchor stranded cotton with some Chinese silk thread for fine details. The background fabric is church linen and it measures approximately 20 x 25 cm (8 x 10 in).

The Malachite Kingfisher (*Alcedo cristata*) is worked in one strand of DMC and Anchor stranded cotton with some Chinese silk thread for fine details. The background fabric is an off-white church linen and it measures approximately 14 x 15 cm (5$\frac{1}{2}$ x 6 in).

The Portrait of Elise was reproduced from a photograph of a Lebanese girl with the permission of the photographer, her brother. It is worked in one strand of DMC & Anchor stranded cotton on a background fabric of fine cambric linen with a batiste backing. It is approximately 19 cm (7$\frac{1}{2}$ in) square.

GUIDELINES

Shading does not always follow straight lines—if you look at a petal, for example, you will see that it most often tapers towards the centre.

To make sure that your stitching follows the direction of your motif you need to use guidelines. Draw these in lightly with pencil.

If you are filling a large area you may find it useful to draw in boundary lines, as shown in the diagram, to help you decide how far to take the colours in each row. Only use boundary lines if you are a complete beginner and feel unsure. (Once you have gained confidence do away with them, as they can limit your eye for subtle shading.)

Remember that these are *approximate* guidelines only and it does not matter if you go over the line slightly or just under. *Do not* stop on the line—you *must* stagger your stitches so that they blend well. This means that your stitches will go outside the boundary line, as shown in the diagram. This is okay—remember that your next row will come back into this row so you still have plenty of space. Don't shorten your stitches to meet the boundary line—just use it as a guide.

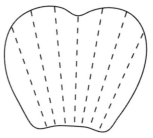

Guidelines for stitching

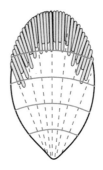

Boundary lines

STARTING AND ENDING OFF

I have found the method demonstrated in this diagram the best way to secure a thread as it does not leave any lumps and bumps. Please don't use a knot!

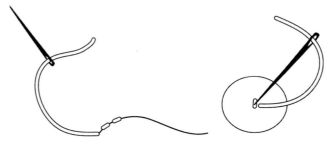

Starting and ending off

If you are starting inside a shape, bring your needle up through the fabric and leave a small tail at the back.

❖ Make a tiny stitch, and then a second stitch at right angles to it and back into the first stitch.

❖ Pull your thread firmly to make sure it is secure and then cut the tail off at the back.

Make sure that this stitch is in a place that will be covered by stitching—just inside the outline is normally good.

If you are starting on a line, make two small running stitches about 10 mm (³/8 in) away from the starting point, then go back to the starting point and begin stitching. The securing stitches will be covered as you work.

To end off, either make another small securing stitch or run the thread under a few stitches at the back.

Outline

It is a good idea to outline your motif with split stitch before filling it with long and short stitch. This gives the shape a nice firm edge and helps to define the motif, especially important if there are lots of different layers (of petals in a flower, for example).

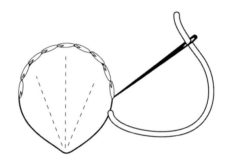

Split stitch outline

Basic long and short stitch
A few hints

Before we start I want to make sure that there is no confusion about the name 'long and short stitch'. It is not, as the name might suggest, one long stitch followed by one short stitch. It is more like staggered satin stitch.

Satin stitch is straight stitches worked side by side to fill a motif, as shown in the upper example here.

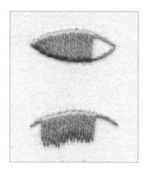

Examples of satin stitch (top) and long and short stitch (bottom)

Long and short stitch is worked in the same way as satin stitch except that the stitches are staggered at the base, as shown in the lower example. Each row enroaches into the previous row. Some stitches must go back into the previous row of stitching, and some forward, creating a staggered blend of stitches.

Be careful not to work the rows in hard-edged bands as shown in the green motif on the right; the stitches should be staggered so that they gently blend into each other, as shown in the green motif on the left.

When stitching the second or subsequent rows of long and short stitch, bring your needle *up* through the

previous stitching and down into the unstitched fabric, as shown in the diagram for row 2 below.

If you go down into the stitching the needle will separate the thread fibres and cause little holes to appear; these make the work look uneven, as shown in the pink and plum motif on the left. Coming up through the stitching anchors the thread, and makes it lie flat, as shown in the pink and plum motif on the right.

Long and short bands of colour

Examples of holes forming in long and short stitch

ROW 1 Stitch staggered stitches across the shape using one strand of thread; these stitches should be full and close together. The stitches should be about 10 mm ($^3/_8$ in) long.

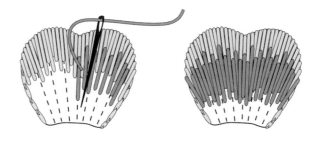

Row 2

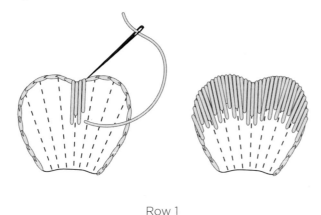

Row 1

ROW 2 Change to the next shade and work the second row. Bring your needle up through the previous stitches and down into the unstitched area as shown. Remember, up, not down.

Don't come up in the end of a stitch—go right back into the previous row (about two-thirds back or more) and make sure to come up through some thread, not in a gap.

Work random stitches across the shape in line with your guidelines and then go back and fill in the gaps.

ROW 3 TO END Continue stitching each subsequent row as for row 2, changing to the next shade of colour each time until the shape is completed. You will naturally reduce the number of stitches as the shape tapers. It is always best to work from the wider area down towards the narrow area as it is easier to reduce the number stitches than to add to them.

Row 3

Practice motifs

Use the motifs provided here for practice. Trace the outline onto a piece of fabric (you can use a good quality calico for this) and follow the directions using the DMC shades provided.

These motifs are designed to guide you through the different shapes and situations you may encounter. Live demonstrations of working these motifs appear on the DVD The Long & The Short of It.

BASIC LONG AND SHORT STITCH
Straight blue petal

DMC thread key

747   3766   597   3810   3809   3808

STEP 1 Trace the outline onto a piece of fabric. Draw in the direction lines with a pencil.

STEP 2 For practice purposes you can work without a split stitch outline as it is easier. Starting at the top of the petal motif, work a row of long and short stitches in 747.

STEP 3 Change to the next shade, 3766, and work a second row.

Petal outline

Step 2

Step 3

STEP 4   Change to the next shade, 597, and work a third row

STEP 5   Continue working rows of long and short stitch to fill the motif, using the next darkest shade each time. Follow the direction lines.

Step 4   Step 5; petal
                      completed

LONG AND SHORT STITCH ON A CURVE
Curved apricot petal

Filling a shape does not always follow straight lines. Sometimes we need to direct our stitches to follow a curve.

The easiest way to get long and short stitch to follow a curve is to shorten the stitches in each row and stitch two rows of each shade. Stitches can only be straight, never curved, so if they are short it is easier to adapt the direction.

DMC thread key

948   353   352   351   350   349

STEP 1   Trace the outline onto your fabric. Draw in the direction lines with a pencil.

STEP 2   For practice purposes you can work without a split stitch outline as it is easier. Stitch a row of long and short stitch in the first shade, 948. Shorten the stitches to about 5 mm ($^3/16$ in).

Curved petal outline   Step 2

STEP 3 Stitch a second row in the same shade, again shortening the stitches.

STEP 4 Change to the next shade, 353, and again stitch a short row.

Step 3   Step 4

STEP 5 Stitch another row in the same shade.

STEP 6 Continue, stitching two short rows in the next darkest shade (352, 351, 350, 349) each time until the shape is filled. Follow the direction lines closely.

Step 5   Step 6; Completed
curved petal

LONG AND SHORT STITCH FOR DIFFERENT SHAPES
Golden flower

Petals that are close together or layered need be defined so that each petal looks as though it is sitting on top of the next. You need to start with the petals that are furthest away and work up to the petals in the front.

Each petal needs to be defined with a split stitch outline and filled with long and short stitch before stitching the next one, so that they look as though they are distinct from each other.

DMC thread key

3823   3855   3854   301   834   832

STEP 1 Trace the outline onto the fabric and draw in the direction lines.

STEP 2 Start with the back petals and work forward. Outline each petal with split stitch first with a medium shade such as 3855. Fill with long and short stitch from the outside edge in towards the centre, using shades 3823, 3855, 3854, 301.

Flower outline

STEP 3 Continue filling each petal with long and short stitch until complete. Fill the centre with French knots using 834 and 832.

Step 2

Completed flower

Petal turnover

One of the problems with a turnover is trying to decide which direction the stitches should go. To do this make a template of the full petal on tracing paper, adding on a bit where the turnover will be. Draw in the direction lines, and cut out the template. Fold over the turnover and you can easily see the direction of the lines underneath. Draw these in.

DMC thread key

3865   153   3836   3041   3740

STEP 1 Trace the outline onto the fabric and draw in direction lines with a pencil.

STEP 2 Stitch the petal in long and short stitch using shades 3865, 153, 3836, 3041 and 3740. Leave the turnover free. Before you stitch the turnover, underline it with one strand of split stitch using the darkest shade, 3740, to create a little shadow.

Petal turnover outline

Step 2

STEP 3 Using the lightest shade, 3865, outline the turnover in split stitch. Now fill it with satin stitches at an angle, following the direction lines. Take the stitches over the edge of the turnover and into the shadow line so that it is just visible.

Completed petal turnover

Leaf

DMC thread key

471   472   469   936

STEP 1 Trace the outline onto the fabric and draw in direction lines with a pencil.

STEP 2 Work the right side of the leaf first. Outline the leaf with split stitch in 471. Using two strands of 471, start at the outside of the leaf and work in towards the centre vein. These stitches will be slightly angled in line with your guidelines. Change to the next lightest shade, 472, and continue blending in until the right side of the leaf is filled.

Leaf outline   Step 2

STEP 3 Fill the left side of the leaf using shades 472, 471, 469, 936. Notice that the dark shades on this side meet the light shades on the other side, which gives the leaf a plump 3D look. To deepen the shadow at the centre vein, work a line of split stitch in the very dark green, 936. This can be continued into the stem

Ear of wheat

This is a good exercise for learning how to fill small shapes. A small shape can be completely, or almost completely, filled with the first row of long and short stitch; or, depending on how small it is, you can fill it with satin stitch, then go back and add the shadows in afterwards on top of the previous stitching. The same principle can be applied to any small shape where you can't fit in rows of long and short stitch.

Because the grains of wheat overlap you should work them as for the petals of the golden flower on page 24, starting with the grain furthest back and working forward. Make sure that the lighter area of each grain meets the shadow at the base.

DMC thread key

676   3828   3781

STEP 1 Trace the outline onto your fabric.

STEP 2 Outline each grain with split stitch in 676, then almost fill each one with long and short stitch using

Completed leaf

Wheat ear outline

the same shade. Split right back into this row, and blend in a few straight stitches in 3828 to create a shadow.

STEP 3 Finally, add a few small stitches at the base in the darkest shade, 3781, to create a deep shadow. You can finish off by adding in a few straight whiskers for each grain in 3828.

Step 2

Completed wheat ear

Berry

Berry outline

This is a good exercise for learning how to stitch round shapes. Draw in precise guidelines to direct your stitching; they should curve around and meet at the centre point of the berry.

DMC thread key

928   932   931   930   3371 (brown)

STEP 1 Trace the outline onto your fabric and draw in precise guidelines.

STEP 2 Outline the shape with split stitch using one strand 930. Start at the outside of the berry and work in towards the centre point, following the guidelines at all times. Using the darkest shade, 930, work stitches around the shape in line with your guidelines. Shorten the stitches to get around the curve.

STEP 3 Every now and then the stitches will need to change direction to adjust for the sharp curve. To help the stitches move around this curve put in a little wedge stitch (see diagram). This will alter the direction of the other stitches and keep them flowing so that they lie next to each other and don't overlap.

Step 2

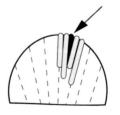

Wedge stitch

STEP 4 Change to the next lightest shade of thread, 931, and work the second row, splitting right back into the first row and staying in line with your guidelines. Continue to work each row with the next lightest shade of thread until the berry is complete. To finish off, make a few straight stitches at the tip of the berry in brown 3371.

Completed berry

LONG AND SHORT STITCH FOR FEATHERS AND FUR

The stitch described here is called irregular long and short stitch because it lets go of all the previous rules. I have demonstrated it on bird feathers, but the same principle can be applied to animal fur or any area where the shading is uneven. The techniques for working smooth and fluffy feathers are quite different, however.

DMC thread key

712   369   564   993   3849

Smooth feathers

STEP 1 Trace the outline onto your fabric and draw in direction lines with a pencil.

STEP 2 To work smooth tail feathers the method is the same as the previous long and short stitch. Outline each feather section separately and, using the colours listed, fill them with rows of long and short stitch at an angle towards the growth point.

Smooth feathers outline   Smooth feathers completed

Fluffy feathers

For working fluffy feathers the method is quite different. Instead of working in rows the colours are placed wherever they are needed. Here you work irregular stitches that blend and encroach into each other, giving the illusion of feathers or fur.

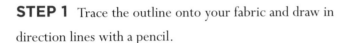

Fluffy feathers outline

STEP 1 Trace the outline onto your fabric and draw in direction lines with a pencil.

STEP 2 Start with the darkest shade, 3849, and work irregular stitches about 1 cm (3/8 in) long, randomly across the outline of the head. The stitches should be feathered out at the top and come in to the point where the feathers grow from the head. It helps to keep in line with the pencil guidelines to establish the direction.

These stitches don't need to be as full and close together as before, because you can go back and fill in any gaps with the next shade. You want to create a light fluffy look, not solid rows.

STEP 3 Change to the next shades, 993 and 564, and continue to add stitches wherever they are needed. Some can go back into the previous row and some can come down into the next row.

Step 2

Step 3

STEP 4 Change to the next shade, 369, and again work randomly across the shape, blending in stitches towards the beak.

STEP 5 Finally blend in the lightest shade, 712, until the shape is complete.

Step 4

Completed fluffy feathers

Stitch glossary

Other stitches can be used as appropriate with long and short stitch embroidery.

BULLION STITCH

STEP 1 Using 2 strands of thread and needle size 9 bring the needle up at A and down at B, then up again at A leaving a long loop.

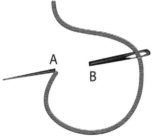

STEP 2 Wrap the thread gently around the needle in an anticlockwise direction the required number of times to create a coil. As a guide, 8 wraps for a short bullion, 18 wraps for a long bullion..

STEP 3 Hold your free thumb over the wraps and pull the needle gently through the coil.

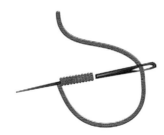

STEP 4 Whilst pulling the thread, gently push down the top of the coil. Adjust coil as necessary until the bullion lies flat on the fabric..

STEP 5 Insert the needle at B and pull through to complete the stitch.

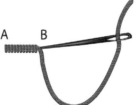

French knot

STEP 1 Using 2 strands of thread, bring the needle up at A. Wrap the thread around the needle once.

STEP 2 Insert the needle tip into the fabric very close to A, but not into the same hole.

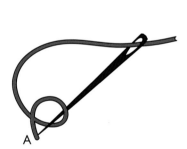

STEP 3 Pull the thread gently but quite firmly to form the knot against the fabric, then pull the needle through to the back of the fabric to complete the stitch.

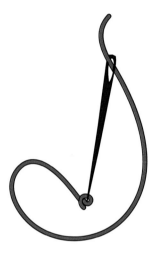

SATIN STITCH

This is a filling stitch used to fill small shapes.

STEP 1 Outline the shape with split stitch. This gives a nice neat, raised edge to your shape.

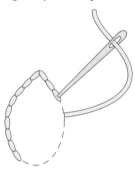

STEP 2 Start in the centre of the shape and work out on either side, angling the stitches across the shape as shown. Work stitches close together across the shape and over the split stitch edge, until it is filled.

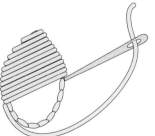

PADDED SATIN STITCH

STEP 1 Outline the shape with split stitch, then work a base of straight stitches across the shape in the opposite direction to the final covering satin stitches.

STEP 2 Work the satin stitch as before on top of the base of straight stitches.

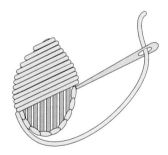

SPLIT STITCH

Split stitch is a variation of a simple backstitch, used to outline shapes and sometimes worked adjacently as a filling stitch for details such as stems. When used as a filling stitch it enables you to shade and change colour within very small spaces, and the results are amazing. This method has become my new preference for filling in smaller details such as stems as it gives more scope for shading in a restricted area.

Commencing with a backstitch, split each preceding stitch with the needle to form the next backstitch.

STEM STITCH

The stitches are worked from left to right and overlap each other, without splitting, to form a fine line. When worked adjacently they can be used to fill spaces such as stems and give a fine cord-like effect.

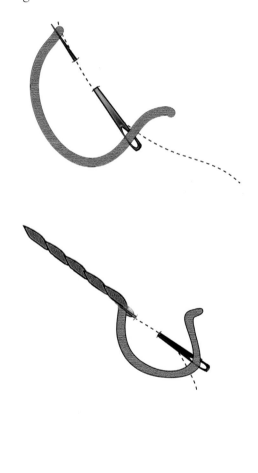

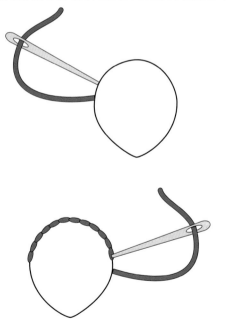

The projects

LEVEL ONE
beginner

These projects are ideal for the beginner with no previous experience. I recommend that you attempt the practice motifs beforehand.

LEVEL TWO
moving on from beginner

These projects help you to develop the technique with slightly more detail than level one.

LEVEL THREE
some experience required

This level introduces birds and flowers in preparation for more intermediate–advanced projects.

1 CERISE ANEMONE

*T*his little anemone flower is the ideal starter project as it is simple yet effective. It would make a wonderful gift finished off as a greeting card, pincushion, scissors fob, needlecase or sachet, or put into a little frame. Here it is embroidered as a cerise-coloured flower, demonstrating the technique of shading from light to dark. The golden yellow anemone in the following project demonstrates dark to light shading.

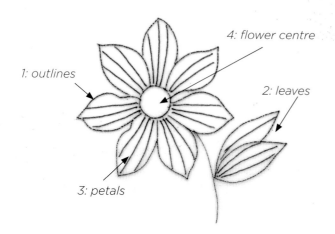

1: outlines

4: flower centre

2: leaves

3: petals

Stitch diagram

Tracing outline

Materials

cotton satin fabric or linen, approx. 25 cm (10 in) square

DMC stranded cotton as listed in key

crewel needle size 9/10

hoop 20 cm (8 in) diameter

Preparation

❖ Iron the fabric to remove any creases.

❖ Transfer the outline onto the fabric.

❖ Draw in direction lines with a pencil.

❖ Mount in hoop or frame, ensuring that the fabric is drum tight.

❖ Use the stitch diagram provided for order of stitching.

DMC thread key

150	165	335	471	472	600
728	782	937	3051	3685	

Method

One strand of thread is used throughout unless otherwise indicated.

1: OUTLINES

NOTE When working stitches down the sides of an elongated shape (such as the leaf and petal) you need to come up on the outside of the split stitch outline and tuck down just inside the outline. These stitches will be almost parallel to the edge, as shown in the diagram.

Working an elongated shape

Outlines key

A 600   B 472   C 471   D 937

❖ Outline the flower in split stitch using one strand A.

❖ Outline the leaves in split stitch using one strand C.

❖ Fill the stem with adjacent rows of split stitch. Stitch one line of D along the pencil mark, then another line in C to the left of this and finally a line of B next to this.

2: LEAVES

Leaves key

A 472   B 471   C 937   D 3051

❖ Fill each leaf with long and short stitch using A, B, C, D.

❖ Use the step-by-step example as a guide. Start at the tip of the leaf and work a row of A.

❖ Stitch a second row in B.

❖ Continue filling the leaf with C and D.

Finally, stitch a row of D at the base of the petal as before.

3: PETALS

1. Start at the tip and stitch a row of A. This row needs to be full and close together, no gaps.
2. Next stitch a row of B. Take your stitches well back into the previous row and bring some of them forward to create a staggered look.
3. Next stitch a row of C as before.
4. Finally, stitch a row of D at the base of the petal as before.

Petals key

A 335   B 600   C 150   D 3685

- ✤ Fill each petal with long and short stitch using A, B, C and D.
- ✤ Use the step-by-step examples as a guide to stitching each petal.

4: FLOWER CENTRE

Flower centre key

A 165   B 471   C 728   D 782

- ✤ Fill the centre circle with padded satin stitch in A.
- ✤ Outline this with a line of split stitch in B.
- ✤ Stitch French knots around the edge of the inner circle using a mix of C and D. Use one strand and two twists.

2 GOLDEN YELLOW ANEMONE

The golden yellow colour shading here demonstrates the technique of dark to light shading, in contrast to the cerise anemone in the preceding project which demonstrates shading going from light to dark.

Materials

cotton satin fabric or linen, approx. 25 cm (10 in) square

DMC stranded cotton as listed in key

crewel needle size 9/10

hoop 20 cm (8 in) diameter

Preparation

❧ Iron the fabric to remove any creases.

❧ Transfer the outline onto the fabric.

❧ Draw in direction lines with a pencil.

❧ Mount in hoop or frame, ensuring that the fabric is drum tight.

❧ Use the stitch diagram provided for order of stitching.

DMC thread key

165	471	524	676	728	729
745	746	782	3051	3052	3053

Method

One strand of thread is used throughout unless otherwise indicated.

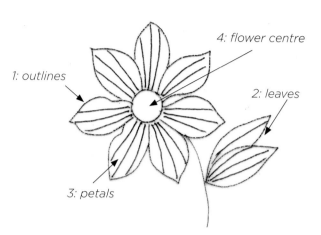

4: flower centre

1: outlines

2: leaves

3: petals

Stitch diagram

Tracing outline

1: OUTLINES

NOTE When working stitches down the sides of an elongated shape (such as the leaf and petal) you need to come up on the outside of the split stitch outline and tuck down just inside the outline. These stitches will be almost parallel to the edge, as shown in the diagram.

Working an elongated shape

Outlines key

A 745   B 3053   C 3052   D 3051

❖ Outline the flower in split stitch using one strand A.

❖ Outline the leaves in split stitch using one strand C.

❖ Fill the stem with adjacent rows of split stitch. Stitch one line of D along the pencil mark, then another line in C to the left of this and finally a line of B next to this.

2: LEAVES

Leaves key

A 524   B 3053   C 3052   D 3051

❖ Fill each leaf with long and short stitch using A, B, C and D.

❖ Use the step-by-step example as a guide. Start at the tip of the leaf and work a row of A.

❖ Stitch a second row in B.

❖ Continue filling the leaf with C and D.

3: PETALS

Petals key

A 746   B 745   C 676   D 729

❖ Fill each petal with long and short stitch using A, B, C and D.

❖ Use the step-by-step examples as a guide to stitching each petal.

❖ The shading is reversed when compared to the cerise anemone; you will be stitching from dark to light instead of light to dark.

1 Start at the tip and stitch a row of A. This row needs to be full and close together, no gaps.

2 Next stitch a row of B. Take your stitches well back into the previous row and bring some of them forward to create a staggered look.

3 Next stitch a row of C as before.

4 Finally stitch a row of D at the base of the petal as before.

4: FLOWER CENTRE

Flower centre key

A 165   B 471   C 728   D 782

❖ Fill the centre circle with padded satin stitch in A.

❖ Outline this with a line of split stitch in B.

❖ Stitch French knots around the edge of the inner circle using a mix of C and D. Use one strand and two twists.

3 SUNSET ALPINE ROSE

*T*his pretty little rose, based on the briar rose Rosa canina, *is portrayed in two different colours—here the soft shades of sunset, vibrant shades of red in the next project. It would make the perfect gift for a friend or relative as it does not take long to stitch. The finished piece could be made up into a scissors fob, pincushion, needlecase, sachet or greeting card, or set in a little frame.*

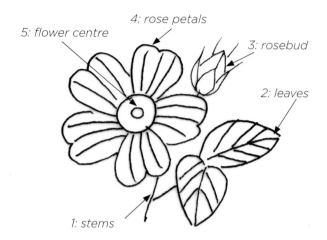

5: flower centre
4: rose petals
3: rosebud
2: leaves
1: stems

Stitch diagram

Tracing outline

Materials

cotton satin fabric or linen, approx. 25 cm (10 in) square

DMC stranded cotton as listed in key

crewel needle size 9/10

hoop 20 cm (8 in) diameter

Preparation

❖ Iron the fabric to remove any creases.

❖ Transfer the outline onto the fabric.

❖ Draw in direction lines with a pencil.

❖ Mount in hoop or frame, ensuring that the fabric is drum tight.

❖ Use the stitch diagram provided for order of stitching.

DMC thread key

352	353	676	734	746	934
951	3011	3012	3051	3829	

Method

One strand of thread is used throughout unless otherwise indicated.

1: STEMS

Stems key

A 734   B 3012   C 3051

❖ Fill the stem with adjacent rows of split stitch.

❖ Work a line of C first, then a line of B, and finally A.
Work two lines of split stitch for the leaf stem in A
and B.

❖ Fill the centre veins with split stitch using one
strand E.

2: LEAVES

Leaves key

A 734   B 3012   C 3011   D 3051   E 934

* ❖ Outline both leaves in split stitch using one strand B.
* ❖ Fill each leaf with long and short stitch on either side of the centre vein.
* ❖ Work from the outside edge in towards the centre vein, using the pictures as a guide. Shade as follows:

Lower leaf

Left side = A, B   Right side = C, D

Upper leaf

Top side = A, B   Bottom side = D

* ❖ Fill the centre veins with split stitch using one strand E.

3: ROSEBUD

Rosebud key

A 353   B 352   C 3012   D 3051

❧ Outline the bud with split stitch in A. Fill with long and short stitch in A and B.

❧ Fill the sepals with long and short stitch in C and D.

❧ Work straight stitches for tips in D, as shown in the detail photo.

4: ROSE PETALS

Rose petals key

A 746   B 951   C 353   D 352

❧ Outline all the rose petals with split stitch in C.

❧ Work each petal in the same way, as shown in the step-by-step pictures. Fill with long and short stitch, working from the outside edge in the lightest shade in towards the centre and the darkest shade, using A, B, C and D.

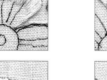

5: ROSE CENTRE

Rose centre key

A 676   B 3829

❖ When the petals are completed, work the centre with French knots in B, using one strand and two twists.

❖ Work straight stitches as shown around the centre in A. Work a few French knots at the bases of the petals in B.

4 RED ALPINE ROSE

This red rose is stitched in the same way as the sunset rose but with different shades.

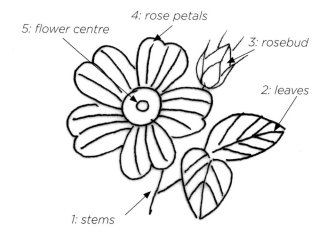

5: flower centre
4: rose petals
3: rosebud
2: leaves
1: stems

Stitch diagram

Tracing outline

Materials

cotton satin fabric or linen, approx. 25 cm (10 in) square

DMC stranded cotton as listed in key

crewel needle size 9/10

hoop 20 cm (8 in) diameter

Preparation

❖ Iron the fabric to remove any creases.

❖ Transfer the outline onto the fabric.

❖ Draw in direction lines with a pencil.

❖ Mount in hoop or frame, ensuring that the fabric is drum tight.

❖ Use the stitch diagram provided for order of stitching.

DMC thread key

321	471	472	469	676	814
816	934	3051	3801	3829	

Method

One strand of thread is used throughout unless otherwise indicated.

1: STEMS

Stems key

A 472   B 471   C 3051

❖ Fill the stem with adjacent rows of split stitch.

❖ Work a line of C first, then a line of B, and finally A. Work two lines of split stitch for the leaf stem in A and B.

❖ Fill the centre veins with split stitch using one strand E.

2: LEAVES

Leaves key

A 472　　B 471　　C 469　　D 3051　E 934

❖　Outline both leaves in split stitch using one strand B.

❖　Fill each leaf with long and short stitch on either side of the centre vein, working from the outside edge in towards the centre vein using the pictures as a guide. Shade as follows:

Lower leaf

Left side = A and B　　　　Right side = C and D

Upper leaf

Top side = A and B　　　　Bottom side = D

❖　Fill the centre veins with split stitch using one strand E.

3: ROSEBUD

Rosebud key

A 816   B 814   C 471   D 469   E 3051

❖ Outline the bud with split stitch in A. Fill with long and short stitch in A and B.

❖ Fill the sepals with long and short stitch in C and D.

❖ Work straight stitches for tips in D, as shown in the detail photo.

4: ROSE PETALS

Rose petals key

A 3801   B 321   C 816   D 814

❖ Outline all the rose petals with split stitch in C.

❖ Work each petal in the same way, as shown in the step-by-step pictures. Fill with long and short stitch, working from the outside edge in the lightest shade in towards the centre and the darkest shade, using A, B, C and D.

5: ROSE CENTRE

Rose centre key

A 676   B 3829

❖ When the petals are completed, work the centre with French knots in B, using one strand and two twists.

❖ Work straight stitches as shown around the centre in A. Work a few French knots at the bases of the petals in B.

5 VIOLET

This embroidery is adapted, with permission, from the painting 'Violet' in Painting Flowers A to Z, *by Sherry C. Nelson MDA, North Light Books, Cincinnati.*

Materials

cotton satin fabric or linen, approx. 25 cm (10 in) square

DMC stranded cotton as listed in key

crewel needle size 9/10

hoop 20 cm (8 in) diameter

Preparation

❖ Iron the fabric to remove any creases.

❖ Transfer the outline onto the fabric.

❖ Draw in direction lines with a pencil.

❖ Mount in hoop or frame, ensuring that the fabric is drum tight.

❖ Use the stitch diagram provided for order of stitching.

DMC thread key

333	469	472	580	581	726
733	742	791	823	830	936
3685	3781	3837			

Method

One strand of thread is used throughout unless otherwise indicated.

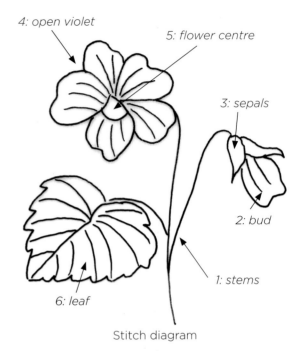

4: open violet
5: flower centre
3: sepals
2: bud
1: stems
6: leaf

Stitch diagram

Tracing outline

1: STEMS

Stems key

A 472   B 733   C 830

- ❧ Stitch the stems in adjacent rows of split stitch, one line next to the other, starting with the main stem.
- ❧ Do one line of A, one line of B, and finally C for the shadow on the right side of each stem.

2: BUD

Bud key

A 3837   B 333   C 791   D 823

- ❧ Outline the bud with split stitch in A. Fill the bud from the tip towards the sepals with long and short stitch.
- ❧ Stitch the first row partly in A, and finish it in B.
- ❧ Work the next row in B. Make sure these stitches encroach right back into the base of the first row.
- ❧ Next add stitches in C, then a few in D for the shadows.

3: SEPALS

Sepals key

A 472   B 733   C 830   D 3781

- ❧ Outline the sepals in split stitch in A. Fill each sepal with long and short stitch.
- ❧ Fill the first sepal on the right with A, B and C.
- ❧ Fill the second sepal on the left with B, C and D.
- ❧ Add some straight stitches along the sides and tips of the sepals in D for details.

4: OPEN VIOLET

Violet key

A 3837   B 333   C 791   D 823

- ❧ Outline each petal in split stitch using one strand B.
- ❧ Fill each petal with long and short stitch, starting from the outside edge and working in towards the centre. Embroider each petal as follows:

  Petal 1 A, B, C, D

  Petal 2 A, C, D

Petal 3 A, B, C, D
Petal 4 A, B, C, D
Petal 5 B, C, D

5: FLOWER CENTRE

Flower centre key

A 726   B 742   C 733   D 3781   E 3685

❖ Fill the triangular shape of the centre with straight stitches using one strand A.

❖ Blend in some stitches in B towards the lower petal.

❖ Blend in some stitches at the top (central point) of the triangle in C and then a few small stitches in D for shadows.

❖ Using straight stitches, make two small tufts on either side of the central point in E.

6: LEAF

Leaf key

A 472   B 581   C 580   D 469   E 936   F 3781
G 733

❖ Outline the leaf in split stitch using one strand A. Fill on either side of the centre vein with long and short stitch from the outside in towards the centre.

❖ **Left side** Stitch 2 rows of A, shortening the stitches slightly to get round the curve of the leaf.

❖ Start blending in B.

❖ Stitch a row of C.

❖ Complete this side of the leaf in D and E.

❖ **Right side** Shade the second side in the same way as the first, starting from the outer edge and using A, B, C, D, E and F.

❖ Work the centre vein in two lines of split stitch, the first using one strand F and the second using one strand G.

6 BURGUNDY ROSEBUDS

*T*his little rosebuds embroidery is the perfect learning tool for shading and has been used in numerous workshops.

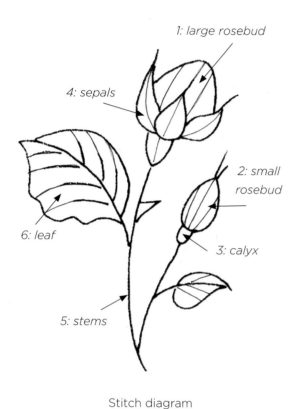

1: large rosebud

4: sepals

2: small rosebud

6: leaf

3: calyx

5: stems

Stitch diagram

Materials

cotton satin fabric or linen, approx. 25 cm (10 in) square

DMC stranded cotton as listed in key

crewel needle size 9/10

hoop 20 cm (8 in) diameter

Preparation

❖ Iron the fabric to remove any creases.

❖ Transfer the outline onto the fabric.

❖ Draw in direction lines with a pencil.

❖ Mount in hoop or frame, ensuring that the fabric is drum tight.

❖ Use the stitch diagram provided for order of stitching.

DMC thread key

154	315	372	370	610	902
935	3011	3012	3021	3047	3722

Method

One strand of thread is used throughout unless otherwise indicated.

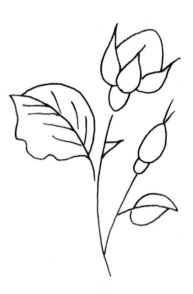

Tracing outline

1: LARGE ROSEBUD

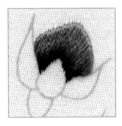

Large and small rosebud key

A 3722   B 315   C 902   D 154   E 3047   F 370
G 372   H 610

1   Outline the tip of the large rosebud in split stitch in one strand A.

2   Continue with rows of long and short stitch in A, B and C.

3   When the bud is complete, create a shadow at the base by blending in a few straight stitches in D.

2: SMALL ROSEBUD

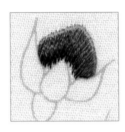 

1   Outline the small rosebud with split stitch in one strand B, then pad across the shape with straight stitches in B.

2   Fill the bud with rows of long and short stitch, starting from the top of the shape and working down towards the base in B, C and D.

3: CALYX

Fill the calyx on the small rosebud with padded satin stitch using E. Make a few straight stitches from the base into the bud using F and G. Work two small fly stitches at the tip of the bud using G and H.

4: SEPALS

Sepals key

A 3047 B 372 C 370 D 610 E 3021

1 Outline the sepals and tips at the base of the large rosebud with split stitch using one strand A.

2 Fill each sepal individually in long and short stitch, from the top towards the base, in A, B, C and D.

3 & 4 Make a few straight stitches at the base, sides and tips of the sepals using E to create shadows. Then outline the calyx with split stitch using A. Pad with straight stitches across the shape in A. Fill the shape with long and short stitch in A and C. Blend in a few straight stitches at the base in D.

5 Finally, take one strand of dark brown E and create shadows along the tips of the sepals and at their bases as shown.

5: STEMS

Stems key

A 3047 B 372   C 610   D 370

✤ Work all stems in split stitch using one strand B. On the main stem work a second line close to the first in C. Fill the thorn with straight stitches in A and the shadow in D.

6: LEAVES

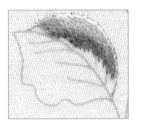 

Leaves key

A 3047 B 372   C 3012   D 3011   E 935   F 3021

1   Outline the top section of the large leaf with split stitch using one strand A. Work a row of long and short stitch in A along the centre and then change to B on either side. Next blend in C.

2   Finally blend in G and E.

2 & 3   Outline most of the edge with split stitch, using one strand E and leaving the edge at the tip unworked. Work a row of long and short stitch using E in the centre and D on either side.

4   Continue working in rows of long and short stitch, using C, B and finally A. Fill the centre vein with split stitch using F.

5   Work the small leaf in satin stitch on either side of the centre vein, using A and B. Blend in a few straight stitches at the base using C. Work the centre vein in split stitch using E.

7 WELSH POPPY

*T*his embroidery is adapted from the illustration of the Welsh Poppy in Redouté's Fairest Flowers, by William T. Stearn & Martyn Rix, A & C Black, London, 1988.

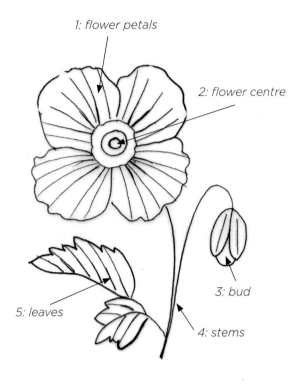

1: flower petals

2: flower centre

3: bud

5: leaves

4: stems

Stitch diagram

Tracing outline

Materials

cotton satin fabric or linen, approx. 25 cm (10 in) square

DMC stranded cotton as listed in key

crewel needle size 9/10

hoop 20 cm (8 in) diameter

Preparation

❖ Iron the fabric to remove any creases.

❖ Transfer the outline onto the fabric.

❖ Draw in direction lines with a pencil.

❖ Mount in hoop or frame, ensuring that the fabric is drum tight.

❖ Use the stitch diagram provided for order of stitching.

DMC thread key

471	472	725	726	727	742
831	832	834	3011	3012	3078
3051					

Method

One strand of thread is used throughout unless otherwise indicated.

1: FLOWER PETALS

Flower petals key

A 3078   B 727   C 726   D 725   E 742

❖ Fill each petal with long and short stitch using A, B, C, D and E, starting at the outside edge and working towards the centre.

❖ Ensure that you bring the deeper shades down the sides where the petals overlap.

❖ Follow the step-by-step photos which guide you through the process of shading each petal.

1   Outline each petal with split stitch using one strand C.

2   Work the first row in A, with a little bit of B near the edge of the overlap as indicated with the arrow.

3   Blend in the next two rows using B and a bit of C near the edge again.

4   Continue blending in C and a bit of D as before.

5   Finally blend in D and E towards the centre.

6   Complete all petals.

2: FLOWER CENTRE

Flower centre key

A 834   B 832   C 831

1 Fill the middle of the flower centre with satin stitch in C.
2 Surround the satin stitch area with straight stitches as shown, using B.
3 Work a few French knots using one strand and two twists in a mix of A and B over the satin stitch centre, and many more at the bases of the petals, as shown.

3: BUD

Bud key

A 472   B 471   C 3011   D 727   E 726

1 Fill the tip of the bud with D and E in satin stitch.
2 Outline the sides of the bud with split stitch in B. Fill with long and short stitch using A, B and C.

4: STEMS

Stems key

A 472   B 471   C 3011

❧ Work lines of adjacent split stitch next to each other. Start on the left with C, then use B and A.

5: LEAVES

Leaves key

A 472   B 471   C 3012   D 3011   E 3051

❧ Outline both leaves with split stitch in C.

❧ Fill each leaf with long and short stitch from the outside edge in towards the centre vein as follows:

❧ **Lower leaf** = A, B, C, D, E

❧ **Upper leaf** top side = B, D; **b**ottom side = B, D, E

❧ Work centre vein in lower leaf in split stitch in E.

8 WILD ROSE

This embroidery is adapted, with permission, from the painting 'Wild Roses' in Painting Flowers A to Z, by Sherry C. Nelson MDA, North Light Books, Cincinnati.

Materials

cotton satin fabric or linen, approx. 25 x 28 cm

(10 x 11 in)

DMC stranded cotton as listed in key

crewel needle size 9/10

hoop 20 cm (8 in) diameter

Preparation

✤ Iron the fabric to remove any creases.

✤ Transfer the outline onto the fabric.

✤ Draw in direction lines with a pencil.

✤ Mount in hoop or frame, ensuring that the fabric is drum tight.

✤ Use the stitch diagram provided for order of stitching.

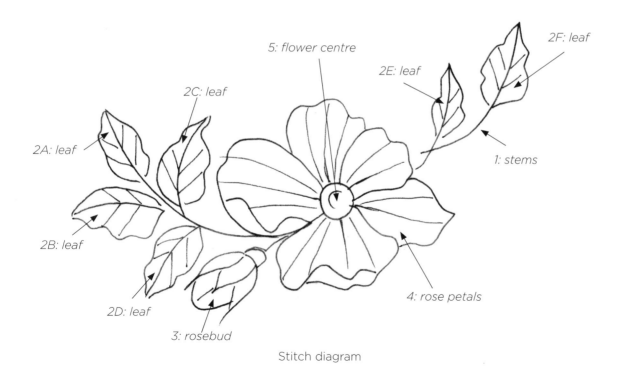

5: flower centre

2F: leaf

2E: leaf

2C: leaf

2A: leaf

1: stems

2B: leaf

4: rose petals

2D: leaf

3: rosebud

Stitch diagram

Tracing outline

1: STEMS

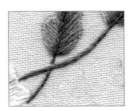

Stems key

A 3045   B 611   C 3781

❖ Embroider the stems with adjacent rows of split stitch using A, B and C.

DMC thread key

223	610	611	729	754	772
3011	3013	3045	3364	3721	3722
3770	3781	3823	3855	3857	3865

Method

One strand of thread is used throughout unless otherwise indicated.

2: LEAVES

Leaves key

A 772   B 3013   C 3364   D 3011   E 3781

❧ Outline each leaf with split stitch in a medium
   shade of green. Fill each leaf with long and short
   stitch from the outside edge in towards the centre
   vein. Refer to the enlarged photos (left) for colour
   placement.

❧ Use the following for each side of the leaves:

Leaf 2A: left side = A, B, C, D; right side = B, C, D, E

Leaf 2B: top = A, B, C; bottom = B, C, D, E

Leaf 2C: left side = A, B, C; right side = B, C, D, E

Leaf 2D: left side = A, B; right side = B, C, D, E

Leaf 2E: left side = A, B, C; right side = B, C, D, E

Leaf 2F: left side = A, B, C; right side = B, C, D, E

❧ Take one strand of E and work the centre vein of
   each leaf in split stitch.

3: ROSEBUD

4: ROSE PETALS

Rosebud key

A 3722   B 3721   C 3857   D 772   E 3013   F 3364

♣ Outline the bud with split stitch using one strand A.
Fill bud with long and short stitch using A, B and C.

♣ Outline the sepals with split stitch using one strand
E. Fill each sepal with long and short stitch using D,
E and F. Work the calyx in E.

Rose petals key

A 3865 B 3770 C 754 D 223 E 3722 F 3721
G 3857

- ❖ Outline each petal with split stitch using two strands of B. Fill each petal with long and short stitch, working from the outside edge in towards the centre and shading with A, B, C, D, E, F and G.
- ❖ Work the back petals first and then the ones at the front. Bring some of the deeper shades—D, E, F, G—up underneath the overlaps as shown.
- ❖ Work the turnovers in padded satin stitch using one strand A.

5: FLOWER CENTRE

Flower centre key

A 3823 B 3855 C 729 D 610

- ❖ Work French knots in the centre using one strand and two twists in A, B and C. Add a few darker French knots around the edge in D.
- ❖ Add a few straight stitches in C from the French knots out into the petals to create stamens.
- ❖ Scatter a few loose knots at the tips of the stamens in B.

9 DAISY SPRAY WITH PINK ROSEBUDS

This embroidery is an adaptation of two Gretchen Cagle designs, 'A painter's legacy' and 'Daisies, leaves and waterdrops', previously published in Heart to Heart ... Forever and Always *and* Heart to Heart ... Sharing the Secrets: Daisies, Leaves & Waterdrops, *Gretchen Cagle Publications Inc, Claremore, OK, 1998, 1999. Permission granted by Gretchen Cagle Publications Inc.*

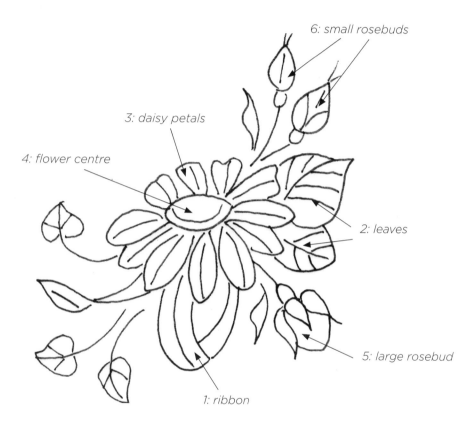

6: small rosebuds

3: daisy petals

4: flower centre

2: leaves

5: large rosebud

1: ribbon

Stitch diagram

Materials

cotton satin fabric or linen, approx. 25 x 28 cm

(10 x 11 in)

DMC stranded cotton as listed in key

crewel needle size 9/10

hoop 20 cm (8 in) diameter

Preparation

❧ Iron the fabric to remove any creases.

❧ Transfer the outline onto the fabric.

❧ Draw in direction lines with a pencil.

❧ Mount in hoop or frame, ensuring that the fabric is drum tight.

❧ Use the stitch diagram provided for order of stitching.

Tracing outline

DMC thread key

151	316	745	746	772	779
819	936	975	976	3011	3012
3013	3047	3727	3348	3371	3827
3860	3861	Blanc			

Method

One strand of thread is used throughout unless otherwise indicated.

1: RIBBON

Ribbon key

A 819   B 151   C 3727   D 316   E 3860

* **Ribbon loop** Start with the back portion of the loop. *Do not* outline with split stitch, start at the base of the loop as shown and work up towards the daisy in long and short stitch. In the first row use two strands of E, and thereafter use one strand as follows: D, C, D, E.

* Next work the front of the loop. Outline the base only with split stitch using two strands B. Start at the wider bottom portion and work up towards the base near the daisy. In the first row use 2 strands of thread and thereafter use 1 strand as follows: A, B, C, D and E.

* **Ribbon tail** Work the back portion first. Do not outline with split stitch. Start at the top near the daisy and work down towards the base in long and short stitch. In the first row use two strands of D and thereafter one strand of E.

* Next work the front portion. Outline the base only with split stitch using two strands C. Work from the wider base towards the narrow tip in long and short stitch in A, B and then C.

2: LEAVES

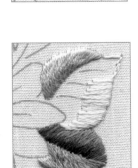

Leaves key

A 3047   B 3013   C 3012   D 3011   E 936   F 779

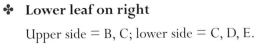

❧ Outline each leaf with split stitch using one strand B.

❧ Fill on either side of the centre vein in long and short stitch from the outside edge in towards the centre.

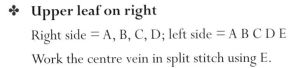

❧ **Lower leaf on right**

Upper side = B, C; lower side = C, D, E.

Work the centre vein in split stitch using E.

❧ **Upper leaf on right**

Right side = A, B, C, D; left side = A B C D E

Work the centre vein in split stitch using E.

❧ **Three small leaves at lower left**

Fill on either side of the vein with satin stitch, using B on one side and D on the other.

❧ Work all the leaf stems with split stitch using one strand F.

3: DAISY PETALS

Daisy petals key

A blanc B 746   C 745   D 3861

- ❖ Outline each petal with split stitch using one strand A.
- ❖ Fill with long and short stitch from the tips in towards the centre, shading with A, B, C and D.
- ❖ Fill the smaller petals with B, C and D only.

4: FLOWER CENTRE

Flower centre key

A 746   B 3827   C 976   D 975   E 779   F 3371

- ❖ Fill the centre with French knots using two strands and one twist. Shade from the top down towards the base using A, B, C, D and E.
- ❖ Finally take one strand of F and scatter a few loose French knots around the base of the centre.

5: LARGE ROSEBUD

Large rosebud key

A 819   B 3727   C 316   D 3860 E 772   F 3348
G 3012 H 3011

- ❖ Outline the rosebud with split stitch in one strand A. Fill with long and short stitch from the tip, using A, B and C. Add a few straight stitches in D at the base to create a shadow.
- ❖ Outline each sepal with one strand E. Fill them with long and short stitch, shading E, F and G. Add a few straight stitches at base with H to make a shadow
- ❖ Fill base with satin stitch in F.
- ❖ Work the bud stems with two rows of adjacent split stitch in F and G.

6: SMALL ROSEBUDS

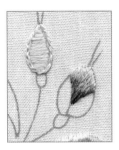

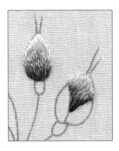

Small rosebuds key

A 151   B 3727   C 316   D 3860 E 772   F 3348

G 3012   H 3011

- ❧ Outline the two small rosebuds with split stitch in one strand B. Pad across the shapes with satin stitch as shown.
- ❧ Fill the larger of the two buds with long and short stitch in A, B, C. On the very small one, use only B and C.
- ❧ Add a few straight stitches in D at the bottoms of the buds to create shadows.
- ❧ Fill the calyces with satin stitch in E. Work a few straight stitches up into the buds using F and G.
- ❧ Work a few straight stitches at the top of each bud with E and G.
- ❧ Fill the two very small leaves with long and short stitch in E, F, G and H.
- ❧ Work the bud stems with two adjacent rows of split stitch in F and H.

10 WILD PANSY

This embroidery is adapted from the illustration of the Viola in Redouté's Fairest
Flowers, *by William T. Stearn & Martyn Rix, A & C Black, London, 1988.*

Materials

cotton satin fabric or linen, approx. 25 x 28 cm
(10 x 11 in)

Anchor stranded cotton as per list

crewel needle size 9/10

hoop 20 cm (8 in) diameter

Preparation

❖ Iron the fabric to remove any creases.

❖ Transfer the outline onto the fabric.

❖ Draw in direction lines with a pencil.

❖ Mount in hoop or frame, ensuring that the fabric is drum tight.

❖ Use the stitch diagram provided for order of stitching.

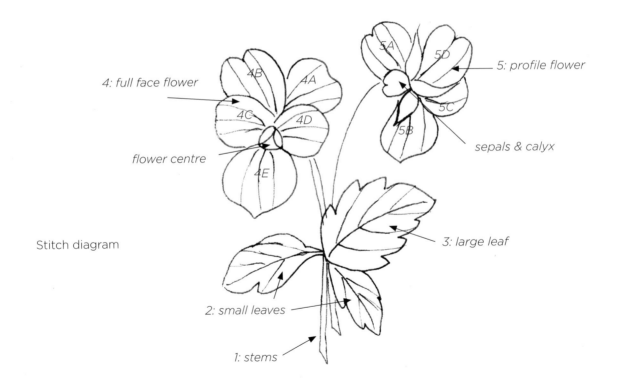

4: full face flower

flower centre

5: profile flower

sepals & calyx

3: large leaf

Stitch diagram

2: small leaves

1: stems

Anchor threads are used in this project. DMC substitutes appear in brackets. Please note that the DMC substitutes are similar but not identical.

Anchor	(DMC)	Anchor	(DMC)
2	(3865)	87	(3607)
88	(917)	92	(3835)
94	(3834)	98	(554)
108	(210)	264	(472)
265	(471)	266	(470)
267	(469)	268	(936)
269	(935)	295	(727)
298	(728)	342	(211)
386	(746)	842	(772)
843	(3348)	844	(3012)
845	(3011)	846	(936)
862	(935)	873	(3740)
901	(680)	1029	(154)

Tracing outline

Method

One strand of thread is used throughout unless otherwise indicated.

1: STEMS

Stems key

A 842   B 843   C 844

- ❧ Fill the stems with adjacent rows of split stitch.
- ❧ Start with the lightest shade and work across to dark with A, B, C, working two lines of each on the left (heavier) stem of A and B and one line of C, and working two lines A and one line of B and C on the right stem.

2: SMALL LEAVES

Small leaves key

A 842   B 843   C 844   D 845   E 846   F 862

- ❧ Start with the smaller leaves at the base. Outline each with split stitch in D. Fill the leaves with long and short stitch as follows:

  Right small leaf Work shading from tip to base using B, C, D, E and F.

  Left small leaf Top half = A, B, C; bottom half = E, D.

- ❧ Fill centre vein of each leaf with split stitch in F.

3: LARGE LEAF

Large leaf key

A 264   B 265   C 266   D 267   E 268   F 269

- ✤ Outline leaf with split stitch in C.
- ✤ Fill with long and short stitch as follows:
- ✤ Upper half = A, B, C, D; lower half = F, E, D.
- ✤ Work the centre vein with split stitch in F.

4: FULL FACE FLOWER

Full face flower key

A 87   B 88   C 94   D 1029   E 92   F 98
G 108   H 342   I 2   J 386   K 295   L 298
M 901   N 873

- ✤ Start with the back petals and work forward.
- ✤ Outline each petal with a medium shade of purple. Fill each petal with long and short stitch from the outside edge in towards the centre as follows:

  Petal 4A: A, B, C, D

  Petal 4B: B, C, D

  Petal 4C: E, F, G

  Petal 4D: E, F, G

  Petal 4E: H, I, J, K, L, M
- ✤ Work the outer sections of the centre in padded satin stitch in I.
- ✤ Make straight lines from the lowest petal in towards the centre as shown in the picture, using one strand N.

 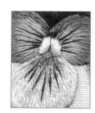

Profile flower key

A 386	B 295	C 298	D 901	E 98	F 108
G 88	H 94	I 1029	J 842	K 844	L 846

❖ Outline each petal as before in split stitch. Fill the petals with long and short stitch as follows:

Petal 5A: G, H, I

Petal 5B: E, F

Petal 5C: G, H, I

Petal 5D: A, B, C, D

❖ Fill the sepals and calyx with long and short stitch using J, K and L.

11 'BURGUNDY ICEBERG' ROSEBUD

This design was inspired by a 'Burgundy Iceberg' rosebud. I have tried to capture the deep burgundy reds and purples that melt into creamy pinks that are so characteristic of this captivating rose.

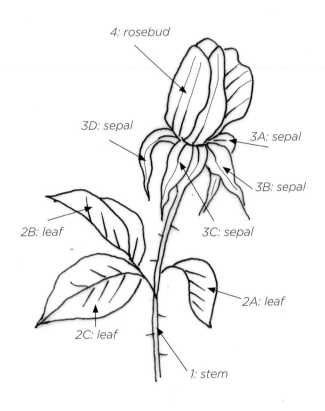

4: rosebud

3D: sepal

3A: sepal

3B: sepal

2B: leaf

3C: sepal

2A: leaf

2C: leaf

1: stem

Stitch diagram

Materials

cotton satin fabric or linen, approx. 25 x 28 cm
(10 x 11 in)

DMC stranded cotton as listed in key

crewel needle size 9/10

hoop 20 cm (8 in) diameter

Preparation

❖ Iron the fabric to remove any creases.

❖ Transfer the outline onto the fabric.

❖ Draw in direction lines with a pencil.

❖ Mount in hoop or frame, ensuring that the fabric is drum tight.

❖ Use the stitch diagram provided for order of stitching.

DMC thread key

150	154	372	772	948	3011
3012	3013	3051	3052	3053	3354
3685	3687	3688	3713	3722	3803

Method

One strand of thread is used throughout unless otherwise indicated.

1: STEM

Stem key

A 372   B 3012   C 3011   D 3722

❖ Fill the stems with adjacent rows of split stitch. Start with the right hand side and work a line of C, then B and finally A.

❖ Take one strand of D and make tiny stitches along the stem for the thorns.

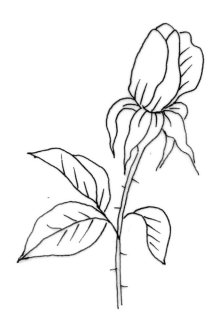

Tracing outline

2: LEAVES

Leaves key

A 772   B 3013   C 3012   D 3011   E 3051

- ❖ Outline each leaf with split stitch using C.
- ❖ Fill each leaf with long and short stitch. Stitch one side from the outside edge in towards the centre vein and then stitch the other side as follows:

Leaf 2A = C, D, E

Leaf 2B: right (upper) side = C, D, E; left (lower) side = A, B, C, D.

Leaf 2C: upper half = A, B, C; lower half = C, D, E. Work the centre vein with a line of split stitch in D.

3: SEPALS

Sepals key

A 772   B 3013   C 3012   D 3011   E 3053   F 3052
G 3051   H 3722

- ❖ Fill the bulb of the calyx at the top of the stem with long and short stitch using B, C and D.
- ❖ Outline each sepal with split stitch in C. Fill each sepal with long and short stitch (shorten the stitches to get around the curves), working from the tip towards the base as follows:

Sepal 2A = B, C, D

Sepal 2B = A, B, E, F

Sepal 2C = A, B, E, F

Sepal 2D = A, B, E, F

- ❖ Create shadows along the tips by adding straight stitches in G, then H.

4: ROSEBUD

Rosebud key

A 948   B 3713   C 3354   D 3688   E 3687   F 3803
G 150   H 3685   I 154

1   Outline the back petal with split stitch in F. Fill
with long and short stitch from the outside edge in
towards the centre in F, G and H.

2   Start at the base of the right front petal and work
up to the tip. Outline with split stitch in C. Begin
with long and short stitch in A and B, and continue
shading with C, D, E, F and H.

3   Fill the left front petal with A, B, C, D, E, F and H.

4   Fill the tip of the rosebud with I.

12 APRICOT DAHLIA

This embroidery is adapted from the illustration of Dahlia simplex in Redouté's Fairest Flowers, by William T. Stearn & Martyn Rix, A & C Black, London, 1988.

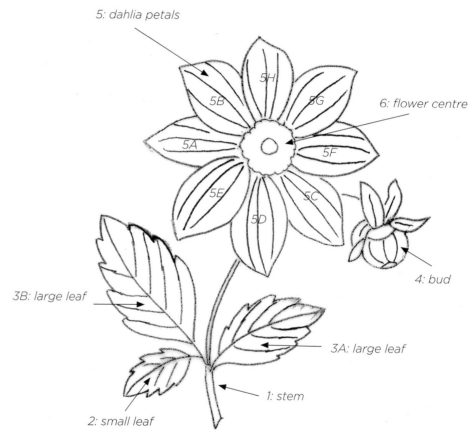

5: dahlia petals

5H

5B

5G

6: flower centre

5A

5F

5E

5C

5D

4: bud

3B: large leaf

3A: large leaf

1: stem

2: small leaf

Tracing outline

Stitch diagram

Materials

cotton satin fabric or linen, approx. 28 cm (11 in) square

DMC stranded cotton as listed in key

crewel needle size 9/10

hoop 20 cm (8 in) diameter

Preparation

❖ Iron the fabric to remove any creases.

❖ Transfer the outline onto the fabric.

❖ Draw in direction lines with a pencil.

❖ Mount in hoop or frame, ensuring that the fabric is drum tight.

❖ Use the stitch diagram provided for order of stitching.

Thread key

Mostly DMC threads are used in this project, with some Anchor colours. Where Anchor threads have been used, DMC equivalents are given in brackets.

DMC

165	350	351	355	729	730
732	733	734	780	783	934
936	967	3341	3770	3822	3824
3830					

Anchor	(DMC equivalent)	Anchor	(DMC equivalent)
259	(772)	265	(3348)
266	(3347)	262	(3362)
218	(501)	683	(500)

Method

One strand of thread is used throughout unless otherwise indicated.

1: STEM

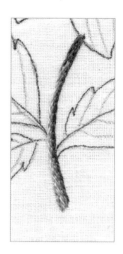

Stem key

A 165   B 733   C 730   D 936

❖ Fill the stem with adjacent rows of split stitch in A,
    B, C and D.

2: SMALL LEAF

Small leaf key

A 733   B 730   C 936   D 934

❖ Outline the leaf with split stitch in B.

❖ Fill the leaf with long and short stitch as follows:
    Upper half = A, B, C; lower half = B, C, D.
    Work the centre vein in split stitch in D

3: LARGE LEAVES

Large leaves key

A Anchor 259	B Anchor 265	C Anchor 266
D Anchor 262	E Anchor 218	F Anchor 683

❧ Outline both leaves with split stitch in B.

❧ Fill on either side of the centre veins with long and short stitch from the outside edge in towards the centre as follows:

Leaf 3A, shading from the top down.

Upper half = B, C, D, E; lower half = A, B, C, D, E, F.

Leaf 3B, shading from the top down.

Left side = A, B, C, D, E, F; right side = A, B, C, D, E, F.

❧ Work the centre veins in split stitch in F.

4: BUD

Bud key

A 3770	B 967	C 3824	D 3341	E 351	F 3830
G 734	H 733	I 732	J 730	K 936	

❧ Outline the round, fat bud with split stitch in B. Fill the bud with long and short stitch using A, B, C, D and E. Work in a bit of F for the shadows. Make sure you follow the guidelines to get the rounded shape. It may be helpful to refer back to the berry practice motif on page 26.

❧ Fill the sepals with long and short stitch using G, H, I, J and K.

5: DAHLIA PETALS

❖ Outline each petal in split stitch using C, and fill with long and short stitch before going onto the next one.

❖ Fill the petals with long and short stitch from the outside edge in towards the centre as follows:

Petal **5A** = A, B, C, D, E, F, G, H

Petal **5B** = A, B, C, D, E, F, G, H

Petal **5C** = C, D, E, F, G, H

Petal **5D** = A, B, C, D, E, F, G, H

Petal **5E** = A, B, C, D, E, F, G, H

Petal **5F** = C, D, E, F, G, H

Petal **5G** = B, C, D, E, F, G, H

Petal **5H** = A, B, C, D, E, F

6: FLOWER CENTRE

Flower centre key

A 3822   B 729   C 783   D 780

❖ Fill the centre with a mix of French knots using one strand and two twists in A, B, C and D, with more of the darker shades in the middle and more of the lighter shades to the outside.

Dahlia petals key

A 3770   B 967   C 3824   D 3341   E 351   F 35

G 3830   H 355

13 RED POPPY

*T*his embroidery is adapted from the watercolour painting Pink Poppy *by UK flower artist Tracy Hall.*

Materials

cotton satin fabric or linen, approx. 28 cm (11 in) square

DMC stranded cotton as listed in key

crewel needle size 9/10

hoop 20 cm (8 in) diameter

Tracing outline

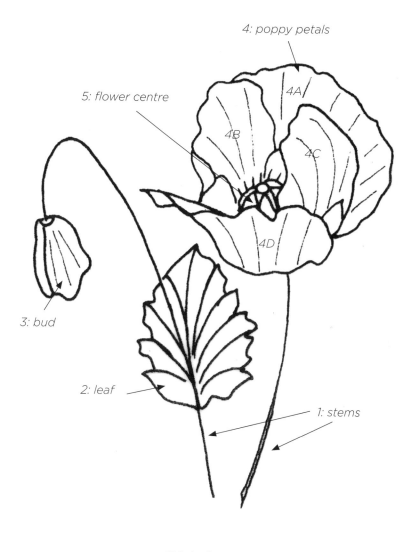

4: poppy petals

5: flower centre

4A

4B

4C

4D

3: bud

2: leaf

1: stems

Stitch diagram

Preparation

❖ Iron the fabric to remove any creases.

❖ Transfer the outline onto the fabric.

❖ Draw in direction lines with a pencil.

❖ Mount in hoop or frame, ensuring that the fabric is drum tight.

❖ Use the stitch diagram provided for order of stitching.

DMC thread key

221	370	372	610	760	761
772	902	3013	3021	3047	3051
3052	3053	3328	ecru	3348	3371
3712	3782	3787			

Method

One strand of thread is used throughout unless otherwise indicated.

1: STEMS

Stems key

A 3047   B 372   C 370   D 610   E 3021

❖ Work the stems in adjacent lines of split stitch. Starting with the lightest colour, work one line in each of A, B, C, D and E.

2: LEAF

Leaf key

A 3047 B 3013   C 3053 D 3052 E 3051 F 3787

G 3021

- ❖ Outline the leaf with split stitch in B.
- ❖ **Right side of leaf**

  Fill with long and short stitch from the outside in towards the centre vein. Work it in two sections:

  Upper part = B, C, D, E, F, G

  Lower part = A, B, C, D, E, F, G
- ❖ **Left side of leaf**

  Upper part = D, E, F, G

  Lower part = A, B, D, E, F
- ❖ Fill the centre vein with split stitch using adjacent rows of G and E.

3: BUD

Bud key

A 772   A 3348   C 3053   D 3052   E 3051   F 3787

G 761   H 3712

- ❖ Work the bud in two sections—first the left, and then the right. Outline each section in split stitch using C. Fill each section with long and short stitch from the outside edge in towards the stem.
- ❖ Left side = F, E, D, C; right side = A, B, C, D, E, F.
- ❖ Blend in a few stitches at the base in G and H.

Poppy petals key

A 761   B 760   C 3712   D 3328   E 221   F 902

G 3371

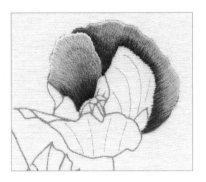

❖ Outline each petal with split stitch using B. Fill each petal with long and short stitch, starting from the outside edge in towards the centre as follows:

Petal 4A = B, C, D, E, F

Petal 4B = A, B, C, D, E, F

Petal 4C = A, B, C, D, E, F

Petal 4D = A, B, C, D, E, F

❖ Work the very dark petal bases by blending G into the bases of the petals.

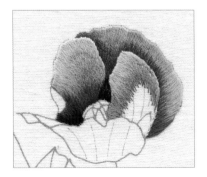

NOTE Shorten your stitches when working around a curve.

5: FLOWER CENTRE

Flower centre key

A ecru   B 3782   C 3787   D 3021

* Work the back part of the centre in the dark shades first.
* Fill with satin stitches using C.
* Next work the triangles in straight stitches in A; make a straight stitch down the centre of each triangle in B.
* Work the centre dot in satin stitch in A and outline with B.
* Take one strand D and work stitches underneath the triangles to create shadows.

6: STEM HAIRS

Stem hairs key

A 372

* Take one strand of A and add delicate hairs along the stems using straight stitch. Vary the angle of some of the stitches to make the hairs look more realistic.

14 LITTLE BEE-EATER

When stitching birds you will need to refer to the instructions for feathers and fur on page 28. Remember that the fuzzy feathers use irregular long and short stitch, which is quite different to the smoother long and short stitch used for flowers. The little bee-eater, *Merops pusillus, is resident in much of sub-Saharan Africa. It is the world's smallest bee-eater, about 15 cm (6 in) long, with a green back and head and yellow and orange underparts.*

Materials

cotton satin fabric or linen, approx 25 x 28 cm (10 x 11 in)

DMC stranded cotton as listed in key

crewel needle size 9/10

hoop 20 cm (8 in) diameter

Preparation

* Iron the fabric to remove any creases.
* Transfer the outline onto the fabric.
* Draw in direction lines with a pencil.
* Mount in hoop or frame, ensuring that the fabric is drum tight.
* Use the stitch diagram provided for order of stitching.

DMC thread key

164	301	435	471	581	611
640	642	644	646	727	728
729	732	822	830	898	920
989	3021	3045	3371	3781	3787
3821	3822				

Method

One strand of thread is used throughout unless otherwise indicated.

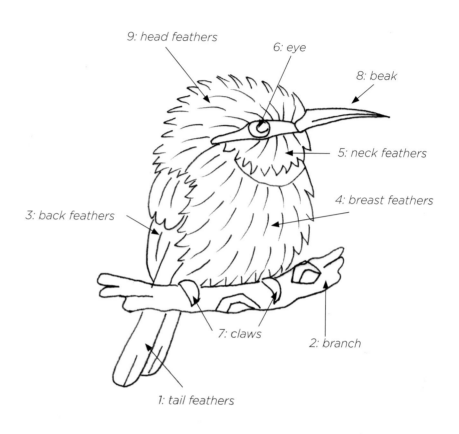

9: head feathers

6: eye

8: beak

5: neck feathers

4: breast feathers

3: back feathers

7: claws

2: branch

1: tail feathers

Stitch diagram

1: TAIL FEATHERS

Tail feathers key

A 3045   B 611   C 3781   D 3021

1   Outline the ends of the tail feathers with split stitch
    in A.

2   Fill the smaller tail feather behind with long and
    short stitch. Work from the outside edge inwards
    using A, B, C and D, approximately two short rows
    of each colour.

Tracing outline

3 Fill the larger tail feather in front with long and short stitch using A, B, C and D, again working approximately two short rows of each colour.

4 Work a line of split stitch between the two tail feathers in E to create a shadow.

2: BRANCH

Branch key

A 644   B 642   C 640   D 3781   E 3045

❖ The shading for the branch does not have to be smooth as you want to create a rough texture.

1 Start at one end and fill with long and short stitch across the branch using A, B, C and D.

2 Continue working along the branch using A, B, C and D.

3 Fill the broken end of the branch with long and short stitch in E and B. Fill the notch on the lower side with straight stitches in E, B and D.

❖ Take one strand D and work in the details demonstrated in the photograph.

3: BACK FEATHERS

Back feathers key

A 989   B 471   C 581   D 732   E 830

1 Work long and short stitch up towards the neck. Start at the base as shown using E.

2 Continue blending in the next shade, D.

3 Continue blending in the next shades, C and B.

4 Continue blending the next shade, A.

5 Blend in shades D and E towards the breast.

NOTE 1 The stitches of the back feathers should encroach into the breast feathers area. This will provide a background into which you work the breast feathers—they will slightly overlap.

NOTE 2 The rows of long and short stitch do not need to be smooth; you can bleed between stitches and roughly blend in the shades to give a feathery look.

4: BREAST FEATHERS

Breast feathers key

A 3822   B 3821   C 729   D 435   E 301   F 920

G 3371

1   Start at the base and work up. Work across the breast with irregular long and short stitch, shading with D and C. These stitches should encroach into each other—some will go into the previous rows and some into the next to give a feathery effect.

2   Continue blending in B and A.

3   Continue blending in B, A, B, C until you reach the neck area.

4   Continue blending in with D.

5   Finally blend in E and F. Add a few short straight stitches in G for the black-brown ring at the base of the throat. The stitches should encroach into the neck area so that you have something to work back into.

NOTE To create curved feathers at the sides work two straight stitches at angles into each other as shown.

Working curved stitches

5: NECK FEATHERS

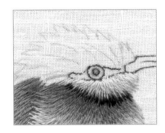

Neck feathers key

A 727   B 728   C 898

1   Blend in a little C to soften the dark neck ring. Continue blending in B.

2   Continue blending in with A until you reach the lower edge of the eye.

6: EYE

Eye key

A 822   B 898   C 3371   D 3021

1   Fill the pupil with satin stitch in C.

2   Fill the iris (around the pupil) with satin stitch in B.

3   Make two tiny little stitches above the pupil (and resting on it) in A. Outline the base of the pupil in split stitch in A.

4   Outline the whole pupil in split stitch in C.

5   Fill the elongated area around the eye with long and short stitch in C and D.

7: TOES AND CLAWS

Toes and claws key

A 644   B 642   C 3021

❧ Work three little bullions close to each other to create the toes.

1 Work the first bullions in A and the third close in B.

2 Work the claws in tiny straight stitches in C.

NOTE It is best to loosen the fabric tension in the hoop to work the bullions for the feet.

8: BEAK

Beak key

A 646   B 3787   C 3021   D 3371

1 Fill the bottom half of the beak with long and short stitch in D.

2 Continue filling the top half of the beak with C.

3 Continue shading with B and A back towards the head.

9: HEAD FEATHERS

Head feathers key

A 164   B 989   C 471   D 581   E 732

1. Start at the back of the head and neck, working irregular long and short stitch towards the beak using A.
2. Continue blending in with B.
3. Continue blending in with C and D.
4. Continue blending in with E. Finally, add a few straight stitches above eye and beak in B.

15 RACQUET-TAILED ROLLER

The racquet-tailed roller, Coracias spatulatus, *a member of the widespread roller-bird family of the northern hemisphere, is found in eastern and southern parts of the African continent—Angola, Tanzania, Botswana, Zambia, Zimbabwe, Mozambique and South Africa. Despite its wide distribution, the species is uncommon, and the small population believed to be ever decreasing. It has been placed on the IUCN Red List of Threatened Species. The long tail feathers which are characteristic of this bird in the breeding season, and give it its name, were unfortunately not visible in the photo I used for reproduction.*

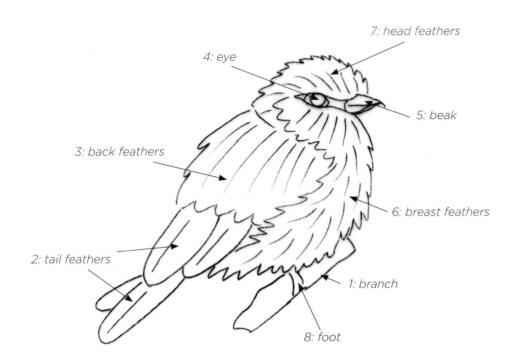

7: head feathers

4: eye

3: back feathers

5: beak

6: breast feathers

2: tail feathers

1: branch

8: foot

Stitch diagram

Tracing outline

Materials

cotton satin fabric or linen, approx. 25 x 28 cm
(10 x 11 in)

DMC stranded cotton as listed in key

crewel needle size 9/10

hoop 20 cm (8 in) diameter

Preparation

❖ Iron the fabric to remove any creases.

❖ Transfer the outline onto the fabric.

❖ Draw in direction lines with a pencil.

❖ Mount in hoop or frame, ensuring that the fabric is drum tight.

❖ Use the stitch diagram provided for order of stitching.

DMC thread key

433	434	435	436	437	519
597	640	642	644	645	747
801	822	839	840	841	842
930	931	3021	3371	3750	3756
3761	3781	3790	3799	3848	3849
3862	3866				

Method

One strand of thread is used throughout unless otherwise indicated.

1: BRANCH

Branch key

A 644   B 642   C 640   D 3790   E 3781

❖ Fill the branch with long and short stitch in A, B, C, D and E.

❖ Work across the branch, shading from the left to right, and allowing the texture to become a little rough and irregular to simulate bark.

2: TAIL FEATHERS

Tail feathers key

A 931   B 930   C 3750   D 3799

❖ Fill the four tail feathers with long and short stitch working from the tail tip in towards the bird.

❖ Fill the back tail feather with long and short stitch using shades C and D. Fill the front tail feather with long and short stitch using shades A, B, C, and D. Start from the tips and work upwards, using A, B, C and D.

❖ Use C and D for the back portion.

3: BACK FEATHERS

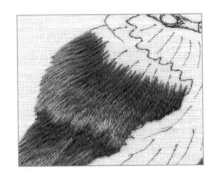

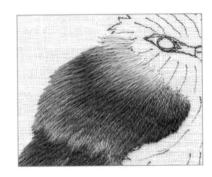

Back feathers key

A 436   B 435   C 434   D 433   E 801   F 839

G 3862   H 841   I 842

❖ Fill the back feathers in long and short stitch, working from the bottom edge up towards the neck in two stages—first the section just above the tail, and then the upper area as far as the neck.

Lower back = A, B, C, D, E.

Upper back = A, B, C, D, E.

4: EYE

Eye key

A 822   B 801   C 3371   D 3021

1   Fill the pupil with satin stitch in C. Fill the iris around the pupil with satin stitch in B.

2   Make two tiny straight stitches above the pupil (and resting on it) in A. Make a line of split stitch along the base of the iris in A. Outline the whole iris with a line of split stitch in C.

3   Fill the area outside of the eye up to the beak in long and short stitch using C and D.

5: BEAK

Beak key

A 645   B 3021   C 3371

1   Working from the tip towards the eye, fill the lower portion of the beak in long and short stitch using B and C.

2   Again working from the tip towards the eye, fill the upper portion of the beak in long and short stitch using A and B.

6: BREAST FEATHERS

NOTE To create curved feathers at the sides, work two straight stitches at angles into each other as shown.

Breast feathers key

A 3756   B 747   C 3761   D 519   E 597   F 3849

G 3848

1   Starting at the base of the bird, work a row of irregular long and short stitch in G.

2   Continue blending in F and E. Bring some of these stitches down into the first row and over the branch.

3   Continue blending in D, C and B. Again, bring some of these stitches down into the previous row, and some across onto the back feathers as shown.

4   Continue blending in A, B, C, D and E until you reach the beak and eye areas.

7: HEAD FEATHERS

Head feathers key

A 3866   B 842   C 841   D 840

❖ Start at the back of the head and work irregular long and short stitches in towards the beak in D, C, B and A.

8: FOOT

Foot key

A 645   B 3371

❖ Take your work out of the hoop to work the bullions for the toes.

❖ Make three bullions next to each other using one strand of A.

❖ First toe = 8 twists

❖ Second toe = 9 twists

❖ Third toe = 13 twists

❖ Secure each bullion with a small straight stitch to keep it in place.

❖ Make straight stitches in B for the claws at the tips of the toes.

SUPPLIERS

Trish Burr Embroidery – South Africa.

Website: www.trishburr.co.za

Email: erenvale@mweb.co.za

Books, kits, DVD tutorial and pre-printed fabric packs. International shipping available.

Mace & Nairn – UK

Website: www.maceandnairn.com

Email: enquiries@maceandnairn.com

Linen, cotton satin fabric plus full range of DMC and Anchor threads. Wendy is always available to help with your individual needs and ships world wide.

Thistle Needleworks – USA

Website: http://www.thistleneedleworks.com

Email: ThisNeedle@aol.com

Linen fabric. Ask for item No 132628 No 401 Linen white. This linen is a milky white and slightly cheaper than Church linen. Please ensure you wash in very hot water to pre-shrink before washing. International shipping available.

Communion Linens – USA

Website: http://www.communionlinens.com

Email: linens@communionlinens.com

Medium weight Irish linen as used for altar clothes etc. This is a superb linen, a little pricey but worth the extra cost for the quality. International shipping available.

Marie Suarez – Belgium

Website: http://www.mariesuarez.com

Email: mariesuarez@skynet.be

This website is in French, but if you email Marie she speaks English and is always willing to cater for your individual needs. Medium weight Belgian linen (300cm wide). This is a fine, good quality linen and because it is so wide it will go a long way. I use a backing fabric with this linen. International shipping available.

Alice Chinese silk threads – China.

Website: http://stores.ebay.com/orientalcultures

Website: www.vendio.com/stores/orientalcultures.

Email: orientalcultures@east-online.com

Alice speaks English and is always very willing to help with your individual needs. She sells over 800 shades of colour in pure Chinese silk. This is the real thing and can be sub divided into ultra fine strands.

Eterna Silk – USA

Website: http://www.eternasilk.com

Email: online email form

The online shop is Yodamo.Inc. They stock a large range of affordable Chinese Silk thread and ship worldwide.

Siesta Frames – UK

Website: http://www.siestaframes.com

Email: online contact form.

Siesta bar frames – these are the most lightweight, versatile frames on the market. They come in different sizes or mixed packs so that you can make up your own size.

The Daylight Company Limited

89 – 91 Scrubs Lane,

London NW10 6QU

United Kingdom

Tel: + 44 (0) 20 8964 1200

Direct Line: + 44 (0) 20 8962 2910

Fax: + 44 (0) 20 8964 1300

Email: audrey.marett@daylightcompany.com

Magnifying lamps.